Soham

in old picture postcards

by
Michael Rouse

European Library – Zaltbommel/Netherlands

For Maxine,
a very special person who first came to Soham in 1983.

Second edition: 1988

GB   ISBN 90 288 3272 6 / CIP

© 1985 European Library – Zaltbommel/Netherlands

INTRODUCTION

For some reason my paternal great grandfather William Charles Rouse left his family home at Great Glemham in Suffolk and arrived in Soham about 1842. Perhaps he set off from the depths of Suffolk to reach the centre of the horse racing world at Newmarket, for in Soham he set up as a blacksmith and veterinary surgeon. He married Caroline Bullman, the daughter of a bootmaker in Pratt Street, and they had fourteen children. One son, Albert, took over the veterinary side for many years living at 'The Limes' in Red Lion Square. Another son, Henry, took over the blacksmithing side and became a member of the worshipful company of farriers. He was my grandfather and had his forge and home in the High Street where he raised a family of eight children.

The Soham he knew so well at the turn of the century had a population of 4,230. A well-known directory described the town as 'long and straggling'. Indeed for many years it seemed little more than one long main road following a ridge of high land halfway between the world famous Newmarket and Ely with its magnificent cathedral. To the south was Soham Mere, a large lake until finally drained in the nineteenth century and all around was rich farmland gradually reclaimed from the marshy Fens since the seventeenth century.

Soham, however, was a religious settlement before Ely. It was founded by Felix — 'the apostle of the East Angles' in the early seventh century. Unlike Ely after the marauding Danes destroyed most of the fenland religious settlements in 870 Soham was not refounded. Nevertheless Soham re-established itself and towards the end of the twelfth century had the church of St. Andrew at its heart.

The town was at a crossing point of the Soham Lode and working boats and barges used the river to transport goods, to the Ouse. Boats also sailed across the Mere.

After the seventeenth century drainage of the Fens Soham became increasingly the centre of a farming community. Every service that farmers required was provided in the town. In the nineteenth century

Soham was remarkable for its number of corn-grinding windmills following the highland through the town. These were in addition to the numerous smaller drainage windmills in the surrounding fenlands.

In 1879 Soham got its railway station on the Ely to Newmarket line and a much wider market was immediately opened up for locally grown produce and Soham was no longer so isolated.

In the years covered by these photographs Soham was also remarkable for its number of public houses — 35 premises were licenced in 1900. Amusement tended to be home produced with sporting clubs, brass bands, a feast and the annual great occasion the Hospital Sunday Parade organised by the Friendly Societies in aid of Addenbrooke's Hospital. From about 1909 Soham, however, had its own cinema in Clay Street. Later in the 1930's there were two cinemas and at one time with the building of the Central Hall, three.

Many came to the town because of its ancient grammar school and there were churches for nearly every denomination. The town has many good and distinguished houses from the late Victorian and Edwardian period, but the essential air was, and still is, of an unpretentious small working town going about its business. Now more quietly because of the bypass opened in 1982.

Far too many people have helped with photographs and information over the years that have contributed to this book for them all to be mentioned. There was my father, Ernest Rouse, who died in 1985 at the age of eighty-two while I was still working on it. I am greatly indebted to Reg and Anita Brown who have the most remarkable collection of Soham scrapbooks and ephemera and have given me unlimited access to their knowledge. I well remember all the talks I had with the late Mrs. Blanche Looker and many others who contributed through my long association with the Village College Soham. I am grateful to everyone who has helped directly or indirectly and hope this collection of photographs will evoke memories and affection for Soham.

1. Bands, banners brigades and new bonnets, all to make the biggest day in Soham's calendar in Edwardian times. While my grandfather would polish his fireman's helmet and join the brigade for the procession through the town, the rest of the family could watch all the parade from the forge in the middle of the High Street. Everyone in Soham it seemed was there and friends from further afield, for in a hard-working life it was a day to look forward to, to celebrate enthusiastically and to remember long afterwards.

2. The Reverend J.R. Olerenshaw, assistant Curate of Soham cum Barway from 1882-1889, wrote in 'The Church of St Andrews, Soham': *In the absence of documentary evidence to support William of Malmesbury's statement that St Felix founded a monastery in Soham and that Lutlingus, a Saxon nobleman, built a church or cathedral, the fact may be recorded of vestiges of buildings and human remains having been discovered on the east side of the main road, and near the site of the Conservative Hall, about 150 years ago and also in 1887.* Again in 1972 when workmen were digging trenches for water mains opposite the church a considerable quantity of human bones were unearthed. This monastery founded in about 647 was destroyed by marauding Danes in 870.

S 1996   PARISH CHURCH AND HIGH STREET, SOHAM.

3. The parish church of St. Andrew owes its origins to Hubert de Burgh, the Chief Justice of England, who granted lands in trust for the church to a man named Ranolph who became the first vicar. Nicholas Ridley was one time vicar of Soham before becoming Bishop of London and being burned at the stake for his beliefs in the seventeenth century. Inside the church is a fine memorial window to the Reverend William Case Morris who was born in Soham in 1864. He became known as the Dr. Barnardo of the Argentine for his missionary work in Buenos Aires where he founded children's homes and schools.

16-8-0?

Churchgate St - Sheen

4. White Hart Lane took its name from the inn standing at the Churchgate Street end. Although the painted sign 'Commercial Hotel – Licensed to let a Horse and Gig' can still be seen on the wall today, the public house has long been closed. Next to the 'White Hart' in Edwardian times was Clark's fancy goods shop. In the distance can be seen 'The Fountain' public house as it had been rebuilt after a disastrous fire in 1900.

5. This is the original 'Fountain' commercial and family hotel photographed in the 1890's when it was run by the Lawrence family. This was a very ancient hostelry, once known as 'The White Lion'. In the lounge is a fireplace dated 1533 and that room was once used as a court. Adjoining the side of the building is the seventeenth century steelyard arm which was used for weighing carts and their produce. It could weigh up to four tons of produce. In the early years of this century Slack and Adams, the auctioneers, ran a cattle market in the yard at the rear of 'The Fountain'.

6. Despite the valiant efforts of the local fire brigade and many volunteer helpers 'The Fountain' was almost completely gutted by fire on the night of 4th May 1900. Fortunately part of the lounge and the adjoining steelyard arm were saved. My grandfather, who was one of the firemen attending the fire, had a presentation half sovereign inscribed with the name and date of the fire mounted for his watch chain. The public house was rebuilt in very similar style to the original as can be seen by comparing the two previous photographs.

S 1995   STATION ROAD AND OLD WEIGHING MACHINE, SOHAM

7. With so much wood in the construction of buildings and open fires the main source of heating it is perhaps no wonder that there were so many serious fires in previous centuries. Whereas 'The Fountain' was rebuilt straight away in the style of the original, it is very unlikely that the adjoining steelyard arm would have been rebuilt if the fire had destroyed it. Fortunately it survived as a fascinating relic of the days before weighbridges. It is one of perhaps only two or three that survive in the whole country. The road is Fountain Lane and the large trees are along the boundary of 'The Place'.

8. 'The Place' was an imposing house with extensive grounds next to St. Andrew's church. The house had been rebuilt after a fire in 1889 and the grounds were a popular venue for garden parties. Indeed this photograph would appear to have been taken on such an occasion. In 1925 it ceased to be a private residence and the whole area, about eleven acres, was sold by auction. It was bought by a private firm who divided the outside of the grounds which were bordered by Fountain Lane, Gardeners Lane and Clay Street, into a number of building plots.

9. In 1928, after the owners had begun to demolish the house and had reduced it to a single-storey building, the parish council purchased it for a pavilion and the rest of the still extensive grounds for a recreation ground. The previous recreation ground having been in Julius Martin's Lane, now the home of Soham Town Rangers Football Club. The pavilion and recreation ground was opened to the public on Whit Monday 1929 when this photograph was taken. The opening ceremony was performed by Lady St. Davids, who can be seen on the left of the speaker, Mr. Ernest Mann.

S 2193   POST OFFICE, SOHAM.

10. The post office occupied this imposing building opposite the church until Lloyd's Bank took the premises in 1924. The post office then moved to Red Lion Square before moving again to its present position in the High Street. Boys anxious to earn a few pence would wait around outside the post office until Mr. Edwards, the post master, would signal them that there was a telegram for them to run to some part of the town. Next to the post office at this time in about 1910 was Pettit's bakery, later Fuller's bakery, and beyond that can be seen Clark's, fancy goods shop, later for many years Staples butcher's shop, and beyond that the 'White Hart'.

11. One of the best known shops during the first part of this century was that of Bobby the chemist. It was well situated in the High Street next to the doctor's house which is seen in the right foreground. Apart from being a chemist Mr. Bobby was also a herbalist. He had a kiln where he used to dry dandelion roots and other plants. The kiln was in Paddock Street just before the entrance to East Fen Common. My father remembered being employed by Mr. Bobby when he was a child of about ten, just before the First World War, to climb inside the kiln to clean it out. John Neville took over the business in 1970. With the railings in front on the left of the view is the house of the Misses Bullman.

12. Some of the thirty-five or so public houses that were a feature of Soham life at the turn of the century began to disappear very early this century. The 'George and Dragon' can be seen in this charming view of a very quiet High Street. It stood between Butcher's outfitter's shop and Henry Rouse's forge.

13. The 'George and Dragon' was demolished to provide a new shop with living accommodation for Leonard's butcher's shop. Mr. Edward Leonard stands in the doorway of his new shop proudly showing what is probably a Christmas display of meat and poultry. The shop front has a splendid gas globe outside it which was much appreciated no doubt by customers as most shops stayed open well into the evening.

14. An incredibly empty High Street again. This time it is photographed in about 1913 or 1914. Following Leonard's example Butcher's now have new premises with more gas globes next door. An empty cart stands outside Rouse's forge as the horse is inside almost certainly being shod. Around this time the cost of putting on four new shoes or plates on a horse was about one shilling and sixpence (7½p).

HIGH ST. SOHAM. 4.

15. The High Street photographed again in late Edwardian times, this occasion looking towards Red Lion Square. On the right hand side can be seen part of Leonard's butcher's shop, then the new double shop with Butcher's, draper and tailor's shop, and Morris', boot and shoe shop. On the corner of Brook Dam Lane is the India and China Tea Company advertising 'Tinned Fruits – apricots, pears, peaches', 'Finest Preserving Sugar' and 'Shaw's Cocoa'. In about 1924 the post office took over the premises.

16. The large house that can be seen endways on to the street was demolished in 1938. It had been the property of Mr. and Mrs. J. Martin and then their daughter Miss Julia Martin until her death in April 1927. The house and outbuildings were demolished to provide a site for the Regent Cinema and car park. Edwards' grocery shop can be clearly seen and standing in front of it a cart with two milk churns on it, a reminder that at this time milk was measured from the churns into customers' jugs.

Red Lion Square, Soham.

95205

17. Red Lion Square was much altered in appearance in January 1921 by the building of the war memorial. Bowman's Stores has now replaced Edwards' shop in a new building which later became the Rendezvous Club. Soham's first cinema was opened in Clay Street just beyond the furthest house that can be seen on the right. It was begun by Mr. Robert 'Nick Nack' Taylor in one of his sheds in about 1909 and lasted until about 1916. It was then replaced by 'The Regal' which Mr. Taylor built next to his Clay Street premises. 'The Regal' lasted until 1952 and from 1939 was in competition with the 'Regent' which stood nearly opposite. The 'Regent', known as the 'New Regent' closed in 1968. The brewery lorry delivering at the 'Red Lion' is from Cutlack and Harlock's brewery at Ely.

18. The cottages in the left foreground were demolished in approximately 1969. Beyond the more substantial houses can be seen trees in the grounds of 'The Place'. When 'The Place' was sold new houses were built on plots there. The white property on the right in the distance was for many years William Doe's stonemason's. This is one postcard in a numbered series of cards published by Lowe of Soham. The same negatives were later used by Hayward's of Soham. The photographer responsible for this outstanding series of town views is unknown to me.

S 8718   THE MOAT, SOHAM.

19. The wooden footbridge over the river which led to the popular walks across moat fields to Wicken. This photograph dating from around 1912 shows the wooden steps at the side of the bridge which allowed water to be drawn from the river in the days before a piped water supply. The wooden bridge was later replaced by an iron one and when the Village College was built on part of the moat fields in 1957 a more substantial new concrete bridge was built.

BROOK DAM, SOHAM

LOWE, SOHAM

20. Brook Dam, where horses could enter the river to drink. A simple turnstyle at the entrance to the railed path restricts its use to pedestrians while halfway along the path are steps for those who wanted to draw water from the river. The river is the River Snail, rising at Snailwell, coming through Fordham, across East Fen Common, before slowly flowing through Soham to Lion Mill. The section through Soham is called Soham Lode and from the mill it takes a direct man-made course to the River Ouse.

21. A pleasant rural scene as the Soham Lode winds on its old course close to Paddock Street near East Fen Common gates. The river course was moved in recent years as a precaution against flooding. Beyond the thatched cottage, now replaced by a modern bungalow, can be seen part of Fyson's paint shop for their engineering works and their unique six-sailed windmill which provided power for their workshop. Fyson's began in 1848 on the Paddock Street site manufacturing windmills and steam engines. Today the firm is still operating from the same site as a leading manufacturer of conveyers.

22. Soham has four commons: East Fen Common, Qua Fen Common, Angle Common and the Shade. They were established in 1664 and at one time 200 acres were allowed to local villagers to graze their stock. Today the commons are controlled by the town council. At one time East Fen Common had many more families living on it and they formed a close community who, it must be admitted, did not always take kindly to strangers.

23. The commons provided lovely walks and recreation areas. On East Fen Common a popular place was Loftus Bridge which crossed the Soham Lode. Cottagers who lived nearby would use the river for washing. One elderly Soham resident recalled: *We used to swim in the river on the Common at the old Loftus Bridge. It was a meeting place for hundreds of children. In the summertime we would bathe and we would swim and the cows had been in there and everything, but we never caught anything. We drank gallons of that old river water, mind you the sewage didn't go into it, and if you got away from the cows drinking spot you were quite alright. We had a proper place where we always went to bathe and swim and paddle.*

24. Soham has an enormously long main road a feature of which is that it changes its name at irregular intervals. From the Shade it becomes Townsend, then Hall Street, Pratt Street, Churchgate Street, High Street, Bridge Street, Sand Street, Fordham Road. On this view the section of the road from the bridge to Red Lion Square is called High Street. On the left can be seen part of the bridge with the top of one of the town water pumps just visible. 'The Ship Inn' on the right at this time, around 1908, was kept by Walter George Cross.

Bridge Street, Soham.

95211

25. Nearly the same view taken perhaps twenty years later and showing several interesting changes. Rose's shop with its distinctive penny farthing weather vane can be seen in the left foreground. Rose's was better known in later years as Summerscale's cycle shop before becoming a garage. When the old shop was removed in July 1971 the penny farthing was taken off and restored to full working order. On the right of the picture the shop window has been replaced in 'The Ship', but further down the street a new shop front has appeared. In Red Lion Square the war memorial can be seen.

26. From the Stone Bridge, this time looking towards Fordham. The sign of 'The Ship' can be seen but not the public house itself. The shop next to the bridge is A.R. Covell's Fancy Bazaar and Confectioners with a sign which says 'Cyclists Rest, teas etc.' On the right can be seen two gate posts giving a drive way entrance down to 'The Moat', while beyond them is the terrace known as Moat Cottages. The road sweeper has paused for a conversation but there appears to be still plenty of work for him to do.

27. Until well into this century there was little of Soham beyond this point on the Fordham Road apart from the cemetery, some windmills and the 'Cherry Tree' public house. The road looks poor and rutted. Indeed recollections of the turn of the century mention the poor state of the roads. They were so churned up by the carts that in winter the water stood so deep on them that many people learnt to ice skate on frozen sections of the main road.

28. Soham was known for its several corn grinding windmills which stood on the ridge of highland which the main road follows. This smock mill was once used by local corn merchants Reuben and John Long and it stood on the Fordham Road south of the cemetery. It stood derelict for many years before being pulled down in 1959.

29. Soham is surrounded by good farming land. Whereas today Downfields mill is surrounded by modern housing, at the turn of the century as this photograph shows, with the horse and binder working, there were fields all around it. The mill was built as a smock mill in the 1720's and rebuilt in 1890 as a tower mill. Known as Pollard's Mill it has in recent years been restored and begun working again although it only has two sails.

S 1998

CHURCHGATE STREET SOHAM.

30. Returning to the centre of Soham and 'The Fountain' in Churchgate Street, the Crown Commercial Hotel used to stand opposite. At the time of this postcard, around 1910, Herbert Robert Hook kept 'The Crown' and as befitted Soham's leading hotel as the sign above the door said: 'Bus Meets All trains.' While the building remains it has not been a public house for some years. Next to 'The Fountain' is Morris' shoe shop, then Desbois, ironmongers, with a large funnel hanging outside, beyond that the iron railings in front of the Wesleyan chapel and the advertising signs on the side of Waddington's grocery shop.

31. A view of Churchgate Street from the other end this time showing clearly 'The Saracen's Head' public house. In the second half of the nineteenth century George Mainprice was a brewer in Soham. He had his premises in Soham at 'The Saracen's Head'. By 1896 Treadway and Percy owned the brewery and 'The Saracen's Head'. In the foreground next to the public house was for many years Reuben Long's corn merchants.

32. Looking further back from Cross Green into Churchgate Street, on the left can be seen the private house, once the home of the Slack family, which became the vicarage for St. Andrew's church in 1954. The former vicarage, next to the church, was converted into flats. On the right of the view can be seen part of the old grammar school buildings.

33. Dick Waddington stands in the doorway of his Churchgate Street shop, probably in the 1920's, with Mrs. Leek, Mrs. Clark, Mrs. Audus, Dolly Moore, Tiny Fordham (later Mrs. Bullman), Gertie Leonard and Mrs. Musk. Richard Waddington had one of the best known and respected businesses in Soham. Someone has written of the family, referring to the times between the wars when there was much unemployment and hardship: *They would take you on trust and all through those terrible years supply numerous families with necessities. I don't remember anyone being denied or badgered for the money – they paid when they could.* Waddington's grocery shop closed in 1976 and became Fine Fare, which closed in 1985.

S 1997 SOHAM GRAMMAR SCHOOL

34. Soham grammar school was originally founded in 1686 and financed by the Free School Moor Charity deriving its money from some one hundred acres of Soham Moor. This building dates from about 1880 and built on an area called the Hempland and the site of the original school. In 1904 the Headmaster, Mr. W.H. Mould, had five assistant teachers, forty day scholars and twenty-two borders. In 1926 the school transferred to a former private house, Beechurst, on Sand Street.

SOHAM GRAMMAR SCHOOL.

35. 'Beechurst' was built by the Morbey family as a private house in 1900. Changing family fortunes led to this, the largest private house in Soham, being bought by the Cambridgeshire County Council in 1925 as the new premises for the old-established grammar school. Generations of pupils became familiar with its narrow corridors, high ceilinged rooms and extensive grounds. The pupils, all boys, came from a wide area around Soham and from Ely, Littleport and Cambridge. Many travelled by train. The school, however, was never very large and all the pupils were able to assemble in the white conservatory clearly seen in this Starr and Rignall photograph of the school. In 1971 the grammar school combined with the nearby Village College to form the new comprehensive mixed Village College with the Beechurst name being restored to the building.

S 1994   **CROSS GREEN, SOHAM.**

36. A beautiful study of Cross Green where Churchgate Street meets Pratt Street. Here stood the town pump which can be seen to the left of the centre of the photograph. Until the piped water supply came in 1923, those who did not have their own wells or pumps relied on public pumps throughout the town, or the river. The town pump stood at the junction of Pump Lane, later renamed Station Road, and Pratt Street. The town pump had two spouts, one for ordinary use and a higher one for water carts. A cap was fitted over the lower spout when the higher spout was needed. The pump was removed in the late 1920's.

37. Certainly by 1918 the Co-op stores seen on the previous view had moved and the corner shop had become Parish's butchers. Later the shop was demolished and replaced by Mrs. Fuller's woolshop and Mr. Fuller's barber shop. In the early 1970's there were further extensive alterations and it became a chemist's shop to coincide with the opening of the new health centre in Soham just off Pratt Street a little further up the street.

38. The coming of the railway brought many changes to towns and villages. In Soham Pump Lane eventually became known as Station Road. This view looks towards Cross Green and shows a thatched cottage pulled down around 1910 and replaced by another thatched house set further back from the road. In the distance can just be seen Johnson's builders yard and sheds.

39. Arthur Long's shop in Station Road with his mother Sarah Ann Long. Mrs. Frances Long started the business by either selling or pawning her husband's coat or cape to buy some sweets which she then sold by displaying them in her front room window. From the profits she bought more sweets and it later became a general stores and was owned by her son John and her grandson, Arthur Long. This photograph taken around 1930 shows that Arthur Long described himself as 'Grocer and Pork Butcher'. The shop closed during the Second World War. Originally the building was thatched with dormer windows, but the exterior was heightened and a galvanised iron roof put on in 1912. The building was demolished in January 1980 to make way for the 'Angel' car park.

40. The coming of the railway to a town usually means some prosperity and new houses on roads near the station. In Soham some fine villas were built along Station Road. The house in the foreground was demolished to make the entrance to West Drive in the early 1960's.

41. Mr. Fuller Brown stands outside his shop at the corner of Station Road and The Piece. This view of his family grocery business was probably taken before 1900. The business went to a Mr. Leonard Rayner for a short while and from him around 1910 to Mr. Horace Taylor. The Taylor family continued the business until the 1950's when the premises were converted into a private house.

42. The railway station, which opened on 1st September 1879 when the Ely to Newmarket Railway line was built, was for many years a focal point of town life. There was a busy bookstall, two waiting rooms, one for ladies and one for gentlemen, with large open fires on cold days. There was a busy goods yard and 'The Crown Hotel' landau carriage met arrivals to the town. The station was torn apart by an explosion on the night of 2nd June 1944 when a train load of bombs caught alight. Only the bravery of driver Ben Gimbert and fireman James Nightall saved total destruction. They managed to uncouple the leading truck which was on fire and pull it away from the rest of the train. They did not manage to get clear of the station before the truck exploded killing fireman Nightall and the signalman Frank Bridges, while Ben Gimbert miraculously survived though badly injured. 523 houses and 22 other premises in Soham were damaged but only two lives were lost. Ben Gimbert and James Nightall were awarded the George Cross. Their action saved Soham from total destruction. The station was never rebuilt and was eventually closed in 1965.

43. A six sailed smock mill stood west of the railway station on the river bank. The mill was taken down in 1926 during the General Strike. As there were no trains running it made it easier for those doing the work to cross the railway lines. Station building and trucks can be seen in the photograph. This area was on the edge of the old Mere which once extended about 1,370 acres. It was a huge inland sea, partly drained in 1666 but still subject to winter flooding through into the nineteenth century. Legend has it that King Canute (1017-1035) crossed the frozen Soham Mere to Ely. A fat fenman, one Brithmer known as Budde or Pudding, walked ahead of the King to make sure that the ice would bear his weight. The local serf was well rewarded by being made a free man.

44. Alfred Clark began his milling business in 1859 with a windmill along the Fordham Road. In 1864, however, he acquired the watermill in Soham which dated from 1811. In 1870 he was joined by Herbert Butcher, a miller from Stetchworth, and they formed Clark and Butcher's. This photograph is a very early one from round 1867-68 showing the old Clark and Butcher's mill.

45. Before the age of great machines with scoops when a river needed dredging out it meant a great deal of work for many men, usually known as navvies which was short for navigators. As the fen rivers are very slow flowing because of the flatness of the land there was much silting up of the river beds and in order to protect the banks and maintain a good flow of water the river was cleared of its mud. Here a gang is photographed near the mill towards the end of the nineteenth century, when horse drawn barges would still be working the fenland Lodes and rivers carrying coal, timber and local produce.

46. A later photograph of the mill from around 1914 showing some considerable increase in size. The water mill had an eighteen-foot-diameter water wheel driving four pairs of stones and an engine driving three pairs of stones. It was later converted to a roller mill. On 12th July 1945 there was a disastrous fire which destroyed the old mill. It was however rebuilt and reopened in 1948. The new mill was called Lion Mill.

47. Clark and Butcher's mill was and still is, a major employer in the town. Many houses were provided in the vicinity of the mill for its workers. Some of the employees are photographed here in 1910. From the left: John Lyon, Roger Clark (senior), Jim Crack, Sam Norman, David Murfit, Art Stimson, Bill Bailey, unknown, Arthur Reeve, unknown, unknown, Bill Newman, Jim Gilbey, George Long, George Murfet, George Gilbey, George Bailey, Rust, Sparks, Art Gilbey, Jonas Long, Charles Bailey and a final unidentified man.

48. George Pollard began a cycle shop in Pratt Street early in this century. Around 1910 he began selling cars and the business developed as a garage over the years. Later known as George Pollard and Son it closed as a family business in 1974. Today a tyre company and other light industries operate from the premises.

49. The house in the left foreground of this view of Pratt Street in the 1930's was the 'Ten Bells' public house at one time, which is why the narrow lane beside it is known as Ten Bell Lane. On the fourth property on the left the sign of the 'Jolly Gardeners' inn can be seen. In 1918 James Steadman, the local chimney sweep who had a sign above his door *James Steadman lives here/ He sweeps chimneys far and near/ If anyones wishes to call/ He'll try to oblige them one and all* became the licensee of the 'Jolly Gardeners'. In 1920 Mr. Steadman's daughter ran a sweetshop in part of the building known as Carrie's shop. Mrs. Parsons as she was later became licensee until the pub closed in 1959. On the side of the house is an ancient sun dial. The tall house in the distance was one of the two doctor's houses in the town until the building of the health centre in the early 1970's.

HALL ST. SOHAM. 2.

50. In the early 1900's between 'The Bushel and Strike' public house seen in the right foreground and Julius Martin Lane, there were four blacksmith's shops and three carpenters. The blacksmiths were William Munns, at what is now No. 40, John Raby at No. 50, the Bridgeman Brothers at No. 56 and Fyson Johnson at No. 2 Townsend. The carpenters were George Shaw at No. 23, the yard in the left foreground, later Fuller and Johnson's, now C.E. Fuller and Co.; Mr. Chips Palmer at No. 54 and Mr. Robert Morley at No. 58. There were three public houses in the same length of road: 'The Bushel and Strike' which still survives, 'The Black Horse' at what is now No. 21 and 'The King's Head' on the site of No. 37. Next to No. 32 Hall Street was Mr. Elsden's hairdressers shop where a child's hair cut cost one penny and an adult's cost two pence the same price as a shave.

A PRETTY SPOT. TOWNS END. SOHAM. No. 131178.

51. The road from Townsend leading to the Fen and Qua Fen Common photographed in the 1930's. 'The Holmes' public house, now a private residence, can be seen. This section of road has recently been named Holmes Lane. Fitches Pit, now filled in, was used for watering horses and horses and carts were driven through it.

SOHAM SHADE SCHOOL 1912

52. The Shade School was built in 1875 and for generations of Soham boys was their school where they completed their education. A few won scholarships to the grammar school, but most left there to start work at the age of thirteen or fourteen. Mr. Fenton, the headmaster sits surrounded by one of his classes. Back row: Bert Peak, Arthur Nicholas, Victor Palmer, Jim Bradley, Harold Wenham, Jack Peacock, Jack Johnson and Hitch. Second row: Herbert Sargeant, Clem Rouse, Claude Fletcher, Cecil Fuller, Les Darnell, Mr. Fenton, Jack Pendle, George Isaacson, unknown, Ellis Howe and Sid Pollard. Front row: Percy Goodin, unknown, George Brown, Sid Audus, Les Goodin and Bert Boon.

53. A class of the infants school in Clay Street photographed around 1916. The school log book for 1916 records: *February 23: A very heavy fall of snow this morning has prevented many little ones coming to school this morning. Nearly half the number on books being absent, registers not marked. Children amused, their clothes dried and then sent home after the storm was over. Children allowed a holiday this afternoon. February 24: A much heavier fall of snow during the night. 37 children present out of 296 on roll. Children allowed to stay as the snow is still falling. Were dismissed at 11.30 a.m. and a holiday given in the afternoon. February 25: Attendance very little better this morning, 101 present at 10 a.m. The roads are in such a dreadful condition, little children were quite unable to walk on them. There has not been such a heavy fall of snow in this locality for many years. The children who came worked on in the usual way but registers not marked.*

54. Employees of Treadway and Percy's brewery photographed before 1914. They are (left to right): Bob Watson, Ike Miller, Sam Martin, Bob Garner, Jim Ames and Jack Gibson. The photograph was taken before 1914 because Jim Ames' arm was injured by shrapnel during the war and left useless.

55. Mr. Albert Murfet, the baker, holds his horse while Henry Rouse, the High Street farrier, shoes it. The photograph was taken in the Murfet's Clay Street yard. Henry Rouse was the son of William Charles Rouse who established himself in Soham as a blacksmith and veterinary surgeon in the 1840's. Henry Rouse first had a forge in Fountain Lane before moving to his father's High Street forge in the early years of this century. Two of Henry's seven sons, William and Ted, carried on the blacksmith's business with their father, then in partnership after his death in 1937. After William's death in 1958 Ted carried on alone until his own death in 1974 which brought to an end three generations of blacksmiths and some 130 years of business in Soham.

56. Practically everything in Soham was linked to the farming community. Fyson's made traction engines which local farmers hired out. Leaving their Paddock Street yard is T2 being driven by 'Brown' Aves of Isleham. It was hired out to him annually for the threshing season. In the background on the street corner can be seen 'The Sportsman' public house, another one that has closed in recent years.

57. Many people worked on the land and the harvest was the all important time of the year. It was a time for hardwork and great celebrations afterwards with barns being cleared for harvest suppers. Here the photographer has recorded a scene of threshing around the turn of the century showing the engine and drum. The name on the farm cart is Aspland, Soham.

58. Agricultural workers take a break to pose beside the engine at St. John's Farm, Soham Fen. In the picture are J.R. Fletcher on the engine, Reuben Fuller, Frank Fletcher, Reuben Fuller senior, Alec Collen, J.R. Crisp and George Malton. Many boys on leaving school took their first job on the land when the farms employed many workers taking on extra on a temporary basis when the season demanded it.

59. The rich farming land around Soham is only workable all year round because of the extensive drainage schemes that have developed since the first draining of the flooded fenlands of England in the seventeenth century. The early engineers, under the direction of the dutchman Vermuyden, cut channels and tried to drain the marshes by gravity to the sea. The rich soil revealed under the waters was a black fibrous peat which shrank when exposed to air. Soon the rivers were embanked to hold their water and windmills were built to lift the water from the land into the rivers and drains. In the nineteenth century steam power was used for drainage and in turn that was replaced this century by diesel and electric pumping stations. During the eighteenth and nineteenth century the Fens were covered in small drainage windmills. These three survivors were photographed in Soham Fen in 1914.

60. Soham Fire Brigade photographed on Bulls Close (Clay Street) in 1897. Back row: F.C. Staples, George Crisp, Alf Palmer, William Isaacson, George Hobbs, Walter G. Cross and Tom Isaacson. Middle row: L. Hook, Henry Rouse, J. Hall and Ellis Staples. Front row: Chief Officer H.W. Townsend, Alf Clark and J. Bridgeman. This brigade, drawn from local shops and tradesmen, would have used a hand-pumped horse drawn engine.

61. The committee for the first Soham Fire Brigade Sports which were held in Liz Tabner's orchard near the site of Lode Close. Back row: William Barber, MacNorton, Leonard, Jim Pollard, Ebenezer Leonard, unknown, George Cousins, Fred Staples, Harry Townsend, George Crisp, Walter Cross, Ellis Staples, Joe Leonard and Edward Wilton. Front row: Fred James, Moore, Alfred Clark, unknown, unknown, Robert Murfet and Jack Hol.

62. Two years after the earlier photograph of the Shade School was taken war was declared against Germany and young men from Soham quickly responded to the call to arms. Clem Rouse, the fourth son of Henry Rouse, joined the Second Battalion, East Surrey Regiment, though he was under age being only fifteen. He saw heavy trench fighting before early in 1915 he was wounded just above the left knee. He returned to the south coast of England for hospital treatment. Infection set in and he died. He was just sixteen. His body was returned to Soham for burial. Many attended the funeral. Some 127 names are recorded on the Soham war memorial and during the four years of hostilities many families suffered similar losses and their loved ones like Clem's older brother Bert were buried near the battlefield in France. A military funeral like this, photographed by Shepherd the Soham photographer, in May 1915 was a rare event.

63. On the 2nd June 1915 Soham saw the funeral of Dr. Arthur Willis. Dr. Willis had lived at the doctor's house in Pratt Street and shared with Doctor Cory the medical care of the people in Soham who could afford the services of a qualified doctor. As can be seen the funeral was a huge and solemn occasion with the police, the church choir, the hearse, the following carriages and people on foot making their way from the church to the cemetery.

64. There was at one time a swimming pool at Clark and Butcher's mill. The changing rooms as can be seen were in an old railway carriage. Swimming sports and galas were held there and there was a strong swimming club. The pool was in use before 1914 and was closed in the early 1930's.

65. Soham Swimming Club was particularly flourishing between the wars. Here the members are photographed in 1924. Back row: Stan Badcock, Alf Palmer, Peter Garner, Ken Elsden, Ernie Rouse, Jack Talbot, Hubert Elsden, Olly George, Fred Turner, Jack Fenn, Harold Peacock and Reg Cook. In front sitting: Eric Mitchell, Elsie Garner, Edna Murfitt, Nora Edwards, Ivy Fordham, Mildred Brown, Dol Fordham and Fred Edwards. There were strict rules for the club. In 1930 membership for adults cost 4/6 a year with under eighteens paying 2/6. All members had to provide their own 'university' costume while the club provided a free badge with the letters S.S.C. in white on a blue background. The ladies and gentlemen had separate sessions for the use of the pool.

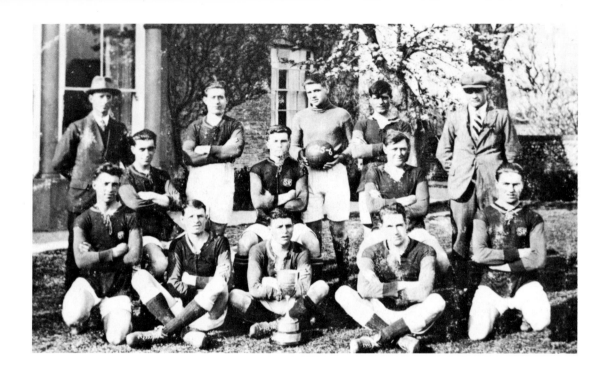

66. Soham Town Rangers cup winning team of 1925-26 photographed outside the home of their President Mr. John Fisk of Brook House in Brook Street. Soham Town Rangers Football Club was formed in 1894. The Rangers played on a field near Brook House but when the Place grounds became the recreation ground, the Julius Martin Lane recreation ground became the home of Soham Town Rangers Football Club. Back row: John Fisk, Peter Garner, George Watson, George Edwards and Ken Elsden. Middle row: Reg Rouse, Alfie Wells and Alf Aspland. Front row: Percy Rust, Maurice Back-house, Charlie Cook, Fred Talbot and Jack Heywood.

67. In 1905 a fund was launched to build a church hall for Soham. At that time the boy's Sunday
school was held in the vicar's barn in Clay Street. In 1912 a site was bought opposite the church in
High Street. It wasn't, however, until October 1929 after the new vicar, the Reverend P.F. Boughey,
had reformed the scheme in 1928 that the project was completed. The cost was £1,920. The new
church hall was opened by Bishop Price, D.D., the Bishop of Ely, in the presence of the widow of the
former long serving vicar John Cyprian Rust who had died on 29th June 1927, after 53 years in
Soham. The Reverend P.F. Boughey is in the centre of the photograph with the piece of paper in his
hand. He served as vicar from 1927 until 1953.

BARWAY CHURCH.

68. An 1888 directory refers to Barway as ...*a hamlet and chapelry belonging to Soham, 3 miles south from Ely and 4 north-west from Soham ...situated in the Fen lands, near the navigable Ouse, River Cam and Soham Brook; it consists only of a few farmhouses... The chapel is a small and plain building, consisting of chancel and nave only, and will seat 130 persons.* St. Nicholas church was probably built in the twelfth century.

69. The inside of the church was as plain as the exterior. These photographs date from the mid-1930's probably shortly after new pews were put in the church in 1933 and renovation work carried out after much fund-raising by the small community. The church ceased being used in about 1962 and was declared redundant and sold in 1972. It was converted into a private house.

70. Barway had a public house, 'The Bull' seen in the background of this photograph. Cooper Ray was the licensee in late Victorian times and the Ray family continued to hold the licence until it closed in 1963. The children in the photograph are gathering behind the union flag for a procession as part of the Sunday school treat.

71. For regular attenders at Sunday schools the annual treat was eagerly awaited. For those who attended the Baptist Church in Clay Street they could enjoy a tour around the town in waggons, drawn by a traction engine, especially as the Superintendent of the Sunday School, Mr. Richard Fyson, was the owner of the engine. Photographed here in about 1923 (the covered trench for the new town water scheme can be seen running down the road) the engine believed to be T 10 is drived by John Robert Fletcher and steered by Frank Fletcher. The trip was a five mile ride via The Cotes to the toll house for milk or lemonade returning home for tea at the Fair Field followed by games. The Baptist Church, erected in Clay Street in 1752 and rebuilt in 1783, had as one of its early ministers, Andrew Fuller, who became known world wide for his preaching and missionary work.

72. The men of the town sit down to a supper and social evening connected with the Foal Show in the Conservative Club in White Hart Lane on 17th March 1909. Soham Foal Show was held in the middle of July and was a popular event until the First World War. It appears that the table in the left foreground is reserved for members of the local fire brigade.

73. Nothing much would have happened in villages and small towns like Soham if it was not for the committee of dedicated workers whether it was the Foal Show or in this case the biggest event of the year, Hospital Sunday. The idea of a fund raising day for Addenbrookes Hospital at Cambridge seems to have begun with the local Friendly Societies and working men's organisations that were usually based on local public houses. The committee photographed here in about 1925 comprises: Back row: S. Peak, G. Peacock and T. Doe. Middle row: W. Cross, A. Palmer, A.E. Murfet, Frost, J. Murfet and S. Bullman; Front row: E. Bradley, Bullman, E. Leonard, H. Townsend, Edmunds, H. Munns and J. Bridgeman. Mr. G. Peacock collected nearly £2,000 for charity in boxes like the one he is holding.

HOSPITAL SUNDAY. SOHAM. 1907. (T. BOLTON.)

74. It seemed that everyone turned out onto the streets of Soham for the carnival procession. A feature of the parade was a float depicting a hospital scene. For many years 'Dot' Munns, who was very small even as an adult was featured on the float. There was more to the occasion than just the parade and collection. The parade heralded the start of the Feast celebrations in Soham in June. As well as the possibility of new clothes for the ladies the men would try and produce a bait of new potatoes and garden peas for the Feast Sunday dinner.

75. An important part of any carnival procession is the music. Before the First World War Soham had two bands. There was the Excelsior Band and the Town Band. In 1921 the two bands came together under the direction of Mr. Frederick Talbot to form the Soham Comrades Band. For fifty-two years Mr. Talbot seen conducting the massed bands in Red Lion Square at the 1921 parade was the conductor of the Comrades Band. Under his direction the band won the East Anglian Championships fourteen times and brought national fame to Soham in November 1938 by broadcasting nationally from the Concert Hall of the B.B.C. They made a second broadcast shortly afterwards.

76. The year is 1927 and Red Lion Square is even more crowded on the day of the parade because the war memorial is in place. The fashions may have changed but it is still the great day in Soham's calendar, just as it was as Blanche Looker described it when she was a child in Edwardian times: *What a day! Everyone out in their best clothes, and the mounting excitement as the time for the Parade drew near. When the sound of the music of the bands drew near, and they marched into view, with their shining instruments, my cup of joy was full. Then the glorious colours in the banners of the various clubs being held aloft. The shining brass helmets of the Fire Brigades and the decorated farm waggon representing a ward of Addenbrooke's Hospital complete with a little bed and its patient and nurses. After that there was the Feast and sports to look forward to. The music from the organ on the Galloping horses, and all the excitement of seeing so many people enjoying themselves. In the evening the Band played again for dancing on an improvised platform. It was magic!*